FIFE'S RAILWAYS REMEMBERED

MICHAEL MATHER

AMBERLEY

To Mum and Dad

Acknowledgements

I am indebted to the following photographers, enthusiasts and collectors, without whose help this book would not have been possible: the 60009 support crew; Jim Balnaves; George Bett; Graeme Blair; Ernie Brack; Bob Bruce; Colour Rail; David Christie; David Crichton; John Cumming; Marshall Dickson; Bruce Galloway; Tony and Nick Harden; Ian Leven; Marilyn Leven; Michael Mason; Graham Maxtone; Bruce McCartney; Ian R. W. McCracken; Peter Rose; Iain A. H. Smith; Neville Stead; and Kenneth J. Williamson.

It was also good to include one of my late father's photographs and a postcard from his collection.

Thanks also go to my daughter, Katie, for proof reading my manuscript and to Graeme Blair for his help.

The Railways of Fife by William Scott Bruce and the Railscot, Six Bells Junction and BR Database websites have all been useful for obtaining information.

Front cover: WD 2-8-0 No. 90199 approaches Lumphinnans East Junction with a Thornton to Alloa freight. (Marshall Dickson)

Back cover: V2 2-6-2 No. 60836 climbs to the Forth Bridge at Jamestown with a Dundee to Millerhill fitted freight. (Marshall Dickson)

First published 2018

Amberley Publishing
The Hill, Stroud
Gloucestershire, GL5 4EP

www.amberley-books.com

Copyright © Michael Mather, 2018

The right of Michael Mather to be identified as the Author of this work has been asserted in accordance with the Copyrights, Designs and Patents Act 1988.

ISBN 978 1 4456 5575 8 (print)
ISBN 978 1 4456 5576 5 (ebook)

British Library Cataloguing in Publication Data.
A catalogue record for this book is available from the British Library.

Origination by Amberley Publishing.
Printed in the UK.

Introduction

The county, or to use its grander title, the Kingdom of Fife, got its first main line railway in 1847–50 with the opening of the Edinburgh & Northern Railway's line from Burntisland to Tayport and Perth, with ferries meeting the trains at Burntisland and Tayport to convey passengers across the Forth and Tay estuaries. With the opening of first the Tay Bridge and then the Forth Bridge, along with subsequent line extensions from Leuchars to Wormit and Burntisland to North Queensferry, rail travel was possible all the way from Edinburgh to Dundee and beyond.

Following the opening of the main, secondary and branch lines during the nineteenth century, Fife was well served by rail – a situation which lasted into the 1960s.

Almost all the railways in Fife became part of the North British Railway, and later the London & North Eastern Railway, before becoming part of British Railways' Scottish Region.

Fife's diverse industries and agriculture provided much traffic for the railway until road transport took over, resulting in the closure of much of the county's rail system.

In this, my second volume on Fife's railways, I have strived to present more historical photographs than in my previous book. I have only been able to do this thanks to the help of a number of mainly local photographers, collectors and enthusiasts, as well as others from further afield. By allowing me access to their collections, I have compiled what I hope is an interesting selection of photographs. Although steam locomotives predominate, first generation diesels are now also passing into history; indeed, the few still working are now into their sixth decade – longer than many steam locomotives lasted – and so they also deserve a place.

Infrastructure, much of which has disappeared or been rebuilt, has also thankfully been recorded on film to be presented here.

Industrial lines, which I only touched on before, get much more coverage, as does some railwayana that has been saved from destruction.

Throughout this volume I have featured a number of photographs of Fife's own A4 Pacific, No. 60009 *Union of South Africa*. The Class 37 hauled Royal Scotsman and the East Coast Main Line HSTs, or InterCity 125s as they were originally called, which are all soon to be history, also feature.

Union of South Africa, or No. 9 as it is commonly referred to, has been a familiar sight in Fife since it entered service in 1937; however, it was not until 1967 that it became a resident following its purchase from British Railways by John Cameron and its move to the Lochty Private Railway, where it worked on summer Sundays until it returned to the main line in 1973.

Since then, having been first based at Kirkcaldy, then Markinch and following a spell at the Severn Valley Railway, Thornton, No. 9 has been kept busy working railtours all over Britain.

All good things come to an end and Mr Cameron has decided to retire No. 9 in 2019 – at the end of its current boiler certificate – and move it, along with his other locomotive, K4 2-6-0 No. 61994 *The Great Marquess*, to a purpose-built museum on his farm.

The Royal Scotsman luxury tourist train has been passing through Fife since its introduction in the 1980s, taking wealthy passengers on a tour of Scotland. For much of this time it has been hauled by Class 37 locomotives supplied by British Railways' Scottish Region, and, following privatisation, EWS and then West Coast Railways. The train is now hauled by Class 66s supplied by GB Rail Freight.

The HSTs have been in charge of East Coast Main Line trains through Fife since 1979 and have proved themselves to be one of the best trains ever on Britain's railways. Soon to be replaced by the new Hitachi Azumas, they won't disappear entirely from Fife as ScotRail are to receive a number of shortened sets from First Great Western, which will work the Edinburgh and Glasgow to Aberdeen and Inverness services.

I hope the reader enjoys what I have presented here. Some photographs are included more for their interest rather than their quality on the assumption that it is better to show something than nothing. I haven't been able to cover everything, but one is limited to the photographs available and, unfortunately, dates for some of the photographs were not available.

So let our journey through Fife begin, starting with the first of three visits to Thornton engine sheds before heading south from the Tay Bridge along the main line, taking in the secondary and branch lines as we come to them.

Michael Mather
Auchtermuchty, October 2017

Two B1 4-6-0s simmer away in Thornton shed yard in the mid-1960s. No. 61347, based at Thornton, would last almost to the end of steam in Scotland, being withdrawn in April 1967, while Dundee-based classmate No. 61263 was withdrawn in December 1966. (David Crichton)

Shortly after purchase from British Railways in 1966, after twenty-nine years of service, John Cameron's A4 Pacific, No. 60009 *Union of South Africa*, stands in Thornton shed yard. A Scottish-based locomotive all its service life, it was initially at Edinburgh Haymarket until being displaced by the new Deltic diesels in 1962. It was then transferred to Aberdeen Ferryhill to work the Aberdeen to Glasgow three-hour expresses. In May 1967, No. 60009 was moved to its new home at the Lochty Private Railway, where it worked for six years before returning to the main line. (Marshall Dickson)

Two photographs of LNER locomotives at Tay Bridge South in the late 1930s. In the top photograph, A3 Pacific No. 2797 *Cicero* is not far from its home shed of Dundee Tay Bridge as it heads an Aberdeen to Edinburgh express, while, in the middle photograph, almost new A4 Pacific No. 4491 *Commonwealth of Australia* heads a similar express. Built in 1937, this Edinburgh Haymarket-based locomotive must have had the day off from its normal Coronation Express duties. (G. Pearson, courtesy of George Bett)

Moving on to May 1987, the National Railway Museum's LNER-liveried V2 2-6-2, No. 4771 *Green Arrow*, is also seen at Tay Bridge South while on its way back to York, having taken part in the Tay Bridge centenary celebrations. The V2s were once a familiar sight in Fife and this is the only one of its class to survive. (Marshall Dickson)

A4 Pacific No. 60027 *Merlin* heads away from Tay Bridge South with an Aberdeen to Edinburgh express in April 1958. Note the HMS *Merlin* plaque affixed to the boiler casing. HMS *Merlin* was a shore-based Royal Naval Air Station at Donibristle in Fife. The plaque was unveiled at a ceremony on the base in 1946. (George Bett)

A BRCW Type 2 (Class 26) pilots a Brush Type 4 (Class 47), at the head of the lunchtime Aberdeen to London express, past Tay Bridge South signal box in September 1973. Double heading was an occasional occurrence with this train as a way of getting the lead locomotive back to Edinburgh. Tay Bridge South signal box is one of only three operational signal boxes remaining in Fife, the others being at Leuchars and Cupar. (Author)

Wormit station in April 1958 sees British Railways Class 4 2-6-4 tank No. 80123 heading a train from Dundee to Tayport. Passenger services beyond Tayport to Leuchars Junction had ceased in 1956 and Wormit station today forms part of Bo'ness station on the Scottish Railway Preservation Society's Bo'ness & Kinneil Railway. (George Bett)

The aftermath of the Wormit rail disaster, which occurred on Saturday 28 May 1955, as photographed the following day. The cause of the accident, which involved Black 5 4-6-0 No. 45458 running tender first and hauling an eight-coach retuning school excursion from Tayport to Dundee, was excessive speed, which caused the locomotive and first four coaches to become derailed on exiting the sharply curved Wormit tunnel. Three people were killed and forty injured of the 539 people on board. (George Bett)

Newport Station

This period postcard, dating from the early twentieth century, shows Newport East station looking towards Tayport. The station, which closed in 1969 following the closure of the line from Wormit, survives and is now a house while the track bed is a road. This station became the terminus of the line in 1966 following the closure of the section to Tayport to make way for the approach roads to the Tay Road Bridge. (Author's collection)

A Metropolitan Camel DMU (Class 101) has just arrived at Tayport station with a service from Dundee in March 1964. By this time, this was the terminus of the line from Wormit that had originally continued on to Leuchars Junction – this being the original line from Leuchars before the opening of the first Tay Bridge in 1878. (Ernie's Railway Archive)

Class 40 No. 40007 climbs away from Wormit with an Aberdeen to Edinburgh express in October 1980. Note the incorrect head code, one of the discs having not been opened. (Graeme Blair)

A1 Pacific No. 60160 *Auld Reekie* passes by St Michaels golf course on the approach to Leuchars Junction with a southbound express in April 1955. This Edinburgh Haymarket-based locomotive was one of a number of this class that carried names associated with Sir Walter Scott's novels. (George Bett)

Moving on to April 2017, and still at St Michaels, a Virgin Trains East Coast HST, No. 43367, slows for the Leuchars stop while working the afternoon Aberdeen to London Kings Cross service – Virgin Trains/ Stagecoach being the current holders of the East Coast franchise. (Author)

Class 4 2-6-0 No. 46464 stands at the Leuchars Junction south bay platform at the head of a train for St Andrews in the late 1950s. This Dundee-based locomotive was affectionately known as the 'Carmyllie Pilot' due to its regular use on the Carmyllie branch line in Angus. It was saved from scrapping by Ian Fraser of Arbroath and is currently under restoration at Bridge of Dun on the Caledonian Railway. (G. Pearson, Iain A. H. Smith collection)

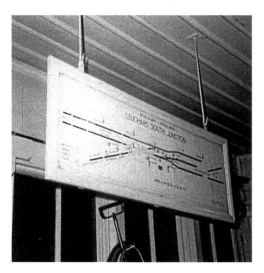

Two photographs taken inside Leuchars South Junction signal box on the night of 4 January 1969 – the date that the St Andrews branch closed. On the left is the track diagram and on the right is the clock, both photographed at the time the last train left for St Andrews – 11.18 p.m. (Bob Bruce)

Guardbridge station photographed from a moving train in the early 1960s. The station, which was opened along with the line in 1852, closed in 1964. Beyond the station can be seen the signal box and level crossing. Out of sight is the viaduct across the River Eden. (Iain A. H. Smith collection)

A scene that has changed out of all recognition shows B1 4-6-0 No. 61263 approaching St Andrews station in the early 1960s with a Dundee to Thornton service. The station site is now a car park while the nearest fields now house more car parking and university buildings. (Iain A. H. Smith collection)

Pounding up the steep gradient from St Andrews, a B1 4-6-0 passes Mount Melville station in the 1950s. Passenger services at this station, along with the next three stations along the line – Stravithie, Boarhills and Kingsbarns – were early casualties. Having opened in 1883 with the opening of the Anstruther & St Andrews Railway, all closed to passengers in 1930. (G. Pearson, courtesy of George Bett)

In this 1965 view, the year passenger services ceased between St Andrews and Leven, the Kingsbarns signalman and the driver of a Metropolitan Camel DMU (Class 101) exchange single line tokens so that the train can proceed safely to the next section. (Ernie's Railway Archive)

A busy scene at Anstruther station sees B1 4-6-0 No. 61330, with its fireman ready to exchange the single line token, arrive with a train from Dundee. Meanwhile, on the other line, J37 0-6-0 No. 64602 stands at the head of a railtour in this view from the 1960s. (Robin Barbour, courtesy of Bruce McCartney)

The East of Fife Railway, which ran from Leven to Anstruther, was fully open by 1863 and served the 'East Neuk of Fife' fishing villages of Elie, St Monans, Pittenweem and Anstruther, all of which were destined to become popular destinations for holidaymakers travelling by train, until road transport took over. The Pittenweem station sign is seen here in the familiar Scottish Region blue. (John S. McCracken, courtesy of Ian R. W. McCracken)

It is 15 July 1966 and the last goods train to travel along the Fife Coast line has just arrived at Pittenweem station behind B1 4-6-0 No. 61347, where it stands among the weeds in the overgrown track bed. A sad sight indeed. (J. B. Duff, Iain A. H. Smith collection)

There may be weeds growing in the track bed, but St Monans station is a tidy sight in this view looking east in the early 1960s. The station stood beside the A917, which crossed the line by the bridge at the end of the platforms. The line closed in 1966, with track lifting beginning the following year, but not before A4 Pacific No. 60009 *Union of South Africa* was hauled along the line to Crail, from where it travelled by low loader to its new home at Lochty. (Iain A. H. Smith collection)

J37 0-6-0 No. 64618 stands in Elie station at the head of a short passenger train. Like most of the stations in the East Neuk, Elie's was on the outskirts of the town – a situation which wouldn't help passenger numbers, especially with the advent of buses and cars. This line's closure was a sad loss, and had it remained open, and with changing attitudes today, it would have been popular with commuters and tourists alike. (Neville Stead)

A Gloucester Carriage & Wagon DMU arrives at Elie station working a Thornton to Dundee service, while J37 0-6-0 No. 64602, seen earlier at Anstruther, awaits its passage. Apart from the local passenger trains, the Fife Coast line had a regular Glasgow to Dundee service appropriately named 'The Fife Coast Express'. (Robin Barbour, courtesy of Bruce McCartney)

The Wellesley Colliery sidings and Methil Docks were a hive of activity with BR, WPR and NCB locomotives at work. Here, in 1969, WPR Barclay 0-6-0T No. 19 heads up the yard with coal for the Wellesley Colliery washer, as an NCB 0-6-0T fitted with a Giesl ejector exhaust propels another load of coal into the NCB sidings. Meanwhile, a shunter, complete with his pole, marches across the scene. (Ian Leven)

WPR No. 19 is seen again, this time passing the Wellesley Colliery washer in 1968. No. 19 was one of a class of five, which were specially designed and built in the 1930s by Andrew Barclay of Kilmarnock for the Wemyss Private Railway. The railway, which remained independent after nationalisation, served all the collieries in the Methil, Levenmouth and East Wemyss area. (David Crichton)

Left: The driver and fireman of WPR Barclay 0-6-0T No. 18 take a break while their locomotive has a drink! (David Crichton)

Right: Photographed in 1969, with piles of coal behind, NCB Hawthorn Leslie 0-6-0T No. 15, NCB Barclay 0-6-0T No. 8 and a BR Class 08 shunter stand in a line in the yard. (Ian Leven)

Left: Taken from the cab of NCB Barclay 0-6-0T No. 10 in June 1970, and with the Wellesley Colliery in the background, an NCB Austerity 0-6-0ST heads towards the camera. (Author)

Right: WPR Barclay 0-6-0T No. 18 storms past Methil West signal box with a trainload of coal for Wellesley Colliery washer in 1969. (Ian Leven)

WPR Barclay 0-6-0T No. 17 propels wagons past Methil West exchange sidings signal box in 1969. The wagon behind the locomotive is carrying coal for topping up the locomotive's bunker during its shift. No. 17 is now preserved at the Speyside Railway, Aviemore. (Ian Leven)

Methil East exchange sidings signal box was photographed in 1968, two years before the closure of the WPR, following the disaster and subsequent closure of the Michael Colliery in September 1967 and the closure of Lochhead Colliery, the last in the area, in 1970. (David Crichton)

Two photographs showing the two types of British Railways Type 2s, with, on the left, a Class 25 in Kirkland yard, Leven, in 1976. The yard is now the home of the Kingdom of Fife Railway Preservation Society. On the right, one of the earlier Class 24s passes the remains of East Fife Central Junction signal box in 1972. This was where the line to Lochty branched off the Leven line. (David Crichton)

Dominated by the nearby distillery and seen here with a fine line-up of bulk grain wagons, Cameron Bridge station, which served the town of Windygates, was the only intermediate station on the Leven Railway, which opened in 1854. This photograph was taken shortly before the station closed in 1969, when passenger services ceased on the Leven line. (David Murray, Iain A. H. Smith collection)

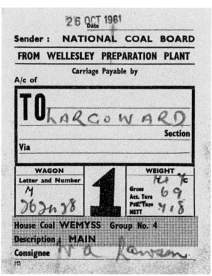

Left: Lochty goods station stood at the eastern end of the East Fife Central Railway. The line opened in 1898 and was goods-only. (Iain A. H. Smith collection)

Right: A wagon label for a load of coal to Largoward, one of three intermediate stations on the line – the others being Kennoway and Montrave. (Jim Balnaves collection)

At Lochty goods yard, a J36 0-6-0 is seen at the head of what appears to be a short brake van railtour. It was intended for the line to continue on to Kingsbarns to link up with the Fife Coast line, but this never happened. Seed potatoes, grain and, up until 1946, coal from Radernie Colliery at Largoward was the main traffic on the line, which finally closed in 1964. (Ernie's Railway Archive)

The last mile and a half of the East Fife Central Railway track bed lay on John Cameron's land, and so, when he purchased A4 Pacific No. 60009 *Union of South Africa*, he had the track re-laid for the loco to operate, which it did on summer Sundays from 1967 to 1972. It is seen on the left departing Lochty, watched by my father, in 1967 and on the right coupled to the ex-Coronation observation coach, again departing Lochty, in 1970. (Author)

When No. 60009 returned to the main line, ex-Wemyss Private Railway Austerity 0-6-0ST No. 16 was acquired to work at Lochty, and is seen here alongside ex-British Aluminium, Burntisland, Pecket 0-4-0ST No. 1. Both locomotives are now at Bridge of Dun on the Caledonian Railway. (Marshall Dickson)

Not having a crane, the volunteers at Lochty utilise an overbridge and a couple of pull lifts to raise the tank on WPR No. 16. (David Murray, No. 60009 locomotive support crew collection)

Photographed on the last steaming day at Lochty in February 1992, before the line closed, newly restored ex-Granton Gas Works Barclay 0-4-0ST *Forth* draws into Lochty station ahead of its naming ceremony. (Author)

The late Davie Murray, who was largely responsible for the restoration of Forth, christens the loco in an appropriate 'Scotch' way. *Forth* can now be seen working at the Kingdom of Fife Railway Preservation Society's site at Kirkland yard, Leven. (Author)

The next station along the main line from Leuchars was at Dairsie and was located about a mile south of the village it served. It was an early casualty, closing to passengers in 1954. Although the station has gone, the loading bank, seen at the far end of the photograph, survives today, and the station yard is now occupied by a coal merchant. (North British Study Group, David Crichton collection, with permission from Mike Jodeluk)

A Brush Type 4-hauled southbound fish train approaches Cupar Beet Factory signal box in 1972, one year after the factory closed. (David Crichton)

Cupar Sugar Beet factory's Barclay 0-4-0ST, No. 1, heads for its shed in this 1966 view. The factory received large amounts of sugar beet by rail during the three-month 'campaign', which ran from October to the end of the year. No. 1 is now at the Caledonian Railway, Brechin. (Ian N. Fraser collection, courtesy of Iain A. H. Smith)

The Cupar cement train derailment on 4 July 1988 caused much disruption, not only to the railway but also to the Cupar to Pitscottie road. Some of the wagons collided with, and severely damaged, the bridge that carried the road across the railway, resulting in it having to be demolished. The cause of the accident was excessive speed and a rail fault, which caused the wagons, hauled by Class 47 No. 47004, to derail. (David Murray)

Two Class 20s with a train of new track panels stand under the temporary walkway which was erected after the Pitscottie road bridge was demolished. (David Murray)

A Cupar station totem, attached to an Edinburgh, Perth & Dundee Railway lamp post. Originally the Edinburgh & Northern Railway, the company name was changed in 1849, two years after the line opened. (George Bett)

On a very dull December day in 1964, Cupar station porter Jimmy Stewart poses in front of English Electric Type 5 Deltic (Class 55) D9006 in Cupar station yard prior to the locomotive's naming ceremony. It was to be named *The Fife and Forfar Yeomanry* as Cupar was the headquarters of this regiment. (Iain A. H. Smith collection)

Class A2/1 Pacific No. 60509 *Waverley* departs Cupar at the head of a southbound express in April 1955. This Edinburgh Haymarket-based locomotive was the first Scottish-based Pacific to be withdrawn, in 1960, after only fifteen years in service. Note that Cupar's centre track was still in place at this time. (George Bett)

The same scene fifteen years later sees Brush Type 4 (Class 47) No. D1973, piloted by BRCW Type 2 (Class 26) No. D5306, at the head of the lunchtime London train at a time when these trains stopped at Cupar. Three years may have passed since the end of steam in Scotland, but the driver, looking back for the right-away, still wears his steam-age dungarees and grease top hat. (Author)

Photographer Alexander Wilson, who worked on the railway at Ladybank, wasn't averse to getting up high to get the photograph he wanted, as these early 1960s photographs taken from a signal gantry and signal post show. In the top view, with the signal box and engine shed behind, an A1 Pacific rounds the curve with an Aberdeen to Edinburgh express, while in the bottom view a WD 2-8-0 brings a long rake of redundant coaches off the Fife and Kinross line past Alexander Bonthrone's Ladybank Maltings and the permanent way yard. (Alexander T. G. Wilson, Iain A. H. Smith collection)

Left: D49 4-4-0 No. 265 *Lanarkshire* stands at the Ladybank Up platform at the head of a whisky train, sometime in the 1930s. This type of locomotive was a common sight in Fife, working goods and secondary passenger services.

Right: C15 4-4-2T No. 67466 stands in the Fife & Kinross dock platform with its one-coach train. When it departs it will propel the coach out beyond the platform before proceeding locomotive-first to Kinross – such was the track arrangement at Ladybank. (Alexander T. G. Wilson collection, courtesy of Iain A. H. Smith)

Quite why a cinema coach and generator van have been shunted into the Fife & Kinross dock platform by J37 0-6-0 No. 64624 in this 1950s photograph remains a mystery, but Alex was on hand to record it anyway. The cinema coach was originally a LNWR twelve-wheel sleeper coach, built in 1907, and is now preserved at the Buckinghamshire Railway Centre, Quainton Road. Above the coach can be seen the Royal Hotel, which was destroyed by fire in 1968. (Alexander T. G. Wilson, Iain A. H. Smith collection)

Twenty years separate these two derailments, which occurred in Ladybank north loop. In the top view, from January 1961, V2 2-6-2 No. 60931 has dug itself into a hole, while in the bottom view, from November 1981, Class 20 No. 20009 has obviously had enough and rolled over! (Alexander T. G. Wilson, Iain A. H. Smith collection)

Ladybank railway workers pose with the army field guns they have just loaded. The guns would have come from the nearby Army Ordnance Depot. Photographer Alexander Wilson is third from the left. (Iain A. H. Smith collection)

It is March 1973 and A4 Pacific No. 60009 *Union of South Africa* has just arrived at Ladybank from Lochty to return to the main line. Once re-railed, the locomotive was moved to Kirkcaldy goods shed, where it was based before going to Markinch the following year. (Alexander T. G. Wilson, 60009 support crew collection)

No. 60009 *Union of South Africa* stands at Ladybank, waiting to take over the railtour it had hauled from Inverkeithing to Dundee earlier in the day. The train had continued on to Perth, Pitlochry and back to Ladybank by diesel. This May 1973 railtour was No. 9's first train after returning to the main line. (Author)

With Ladybank Junction signal box in the foreground, and shortly before pilots were withdrawn from Ladybank, a Class 08 shunter and brake van stand at what was the coaling stage in front of Ladybank engine shed in January 1973. (Author)

My daughter, complete with an 'Ian Allan Combined Volume', sits on one of Ladybank Junction's fine platform seats in July 1984. Most of Fife's stations had this style of seat, complete with the station name. (Author)

In original livery, an InterCity 125 powers round the curve at Ladybank in July 1984, on its way south. By this time the signal box and engine shed had been demolished, leaving only the wagon repair shops, visible beyond the junction. (Author)

The Royal Scotsman tourist train originally consisted of BR Mk 1 and historic coaching stock, and is seen here behind Class 37 No. 37261 *Caithness* when about to reverse into Ladybank yard, where it will spend the night. A small platform was built for passengers to alight and they were piped off by a local piper. The now-demolished wagon repair shops are behind the locomotive in this June 1987 view. (Author)

Left top and bottom: Both sides of a ticket issued on the last day of passenger services between Ladybank and Perth, 17 September 1955. (Marilyn Leven collection)

Right: On a sunny October day in 1970, a Class 20 approaches Ladybank from Perth with a short train of empty mineral wagons. (Author)

An English Electric Type 4 (Class 40) passes the site of Collessie station in the early 1960s with a diverted northbound express. Whether it was the Glenfarg or the Tay Bridge to Ladybank routes that were closed has not been recorded, but this would be a rare passenger train sighting on this line at this time. (Alexander T. G. Wilson, Iain A. H. Smith collection)

A rather grainy shot of Glenburnie Junction, looking south, showing the Newburgh & North of Fife line turning off to the left. This photograph must have been taken before 1933 when the Ladybank to Bridge of Earn Junction line was singled, with the exception of the Newburgh to Glenburnie Junction section. (Graeme Blair collection)

Strathclyde PTE-liveried Class 107 DMU No. 107738 passes the site of Glenburnie Junction in July 1990 while working an Edinburgh to Perth service. (Graeme Blair)

BRITISH RAILWAYS *Glenburnie Jct* Signal Box **UP LINE** 15 *February* 1960 BR. 24665

Monday

		REAR SECTION							ADVANCE SECTION						BLOCK BACK SIGNAL			
		IS LINE CLEAR							IS LINE CLEAR									
Description how Signalled	Circuit Received	Received but NOT Accepted	Accepted under Regulation 5	Accepted under Regulation 3	Train Entering Section Received	Number of Engine	Train Arrived	Train Departed or Passed	Train Out of Section, Signal Given	Offered but NOT Accepted	Accepted under Regulation 5	Accepted under Regulation 3	Train Entering Section Received	Train Out of Section, Signal Received	Time Given or Received	Obstruction Removed Signal Given or Received	Time Train is ready to Depart	REMARKS
		H. M.	H. M.	H. M.	H. M.		H. M.	H. M.	H. M.	H. M.	H. M.	H. M.	H. M.	H. M.	H. M.	H. M.	H. M	

Smith on 12·46 P

3·1·1		12.39	12.40				12.46		12.40	12.46	1·7							10·45
3·1·1		12.56	1·7				1·11		1·7	1·11	1·21							12.55
4·1		4.34	4.52				4.50		4.52	4.58	5.12							4.5
7·55	To Ladybank ...													To Newburgh				8·15 P

Smith off 8·25 P

Tuesday 16 February

5·55	To Ladybank ...										Newburgh	5·30 ...						
5·55	From ...										6·10 ...							
1·4		9	9·5		9·14		9·28		9·26	9·26	9·47							524
	Fireman John Wilson 9·19 Rule 55 Up Line																	65964
3·1·1		9·52	9·52				10·3		9·56	10·3	10·18							9·30

Smith on 12·40 P

3		12.40	12.40				12.53		12.40	12.53	1·16							10·45
3·1·1		12.53	1·1		1·5		1·17		1·16	1·16	1·29							12·55
	Smith Rule 55					1·10 pm		Up Yard				58						60027

An excerpt from the last Glenburnie Junction signal box train register, for 15 February 1960, with signalman David Smith on duty. The box closed on 22 April 1960 when the section of the North of Fife line from Glenburnie Junction to Lindores closed. Note the two rule 55 entries (train waiting on main line) signed by the firemen and the locomotives' numbers noted, one a distinguished visitor in the shape of A4 Pacific No. 60027 *Merlin*. (Graeme Blair collection)

ScotRail-liveried Class 47 No. 47711 *Greyfriars Bobby* heads south at the site of Glenburnie Junction with an Inverness to Edinburgh service in June 1990. In the distance is Bell Brothers' Clatchard Craig Quarry, which used to supply thousands of tons of ballast to the railway. (Graeme Blair)

Looking very smart, two West Coast Railways Class 37s, Nos 37197 *Loch Laidon* and 37261 *Loch Arkaig*, pass Glenburnie in July 2005 with the northbound Royal Scotsman, now all comprised of modified BR Mk 1 stock. (Author)

In 1990, and again in 1993, British Railways' Scottish Region hired A4 Pacific No. 60009 *Union of South Africa* to haul a number of crew-training trains. Running weekdays daily for a month each time, this provided the railway with the steam drivers and firemen it needed, as most of the existing steam crews were approaching retirement. No. 9 is seen here on one of these trains in March 1990 while running as *Osprey* – its originally intended name, but never carried in service – climbing past Clatchard Craig Quarry. (Graeme Blair)

With the two preserved ex-Caledonian Railway coaches behind, North British Railway D34 Glen Class 4-4-0 No. 256 *Glen Douglas* heads the June 1960 SLS/RCTS Scottish railtour through Newburgh station. This five-day tour visited many soon to be closed lines in Scotland, using a variety of locomotives. *Glen Douglas* is now in the Riverside Museum, Glasgow. (Colour Rail)

B1 4-6-0 No. 61172 pauses at Newburgh station while hauling a St Andrews University railtour in October 1960. The tour had visited a number of lines in Fife, including the Fife Coast & Leslie, and also went on to visit the North of Fife line from Dundee behind Standard Class 4 2-6-4T No. 80090 before returning to St Andrews. (Alexander T. G. Wilson, Iain A. H. Smith collection)

Left: An unidentified Caledonian 0-4-4T heads a two-coach Perth to Dundee train across the A92 at Luthrie on the Newburgh & North of Fife line. This early BR photograph must have been taken before 1951, when passenger services were withdrawn from this line. (Iain A. H. Smith collection)

Right: J39 0-6-0 No. 64786 heads a BLS/SLS Scottish Rambler at Kilmany station in April 1962, two years before the line closed. This is thought to be the last passenger working on the North of Fife line. (Alexander T. G. Wilson, Iain A. H. Smith collection)

Passengers explore the station in this second view of the BLS/SLS special at Kilmany. Eleven years have passed since passenger services ceased, but signs, seats, lamps and so on are still in place. This line had a very short life, opening in 1909 and closing in 1964. It was originally intended to be double track, but it remained single throughout. (Alexander T. G. Wilson, Iain A. H. Smith collection)

WD 2-8-0 No. 90049, with brake van, heads a long rake of assorted styles of redundant coaches along the Fife & Kinross Railway and past Monkstown, Ladybank. The line, which opened in 1857/58, ran from Ladybank to Kinross. The section from Auchtermuchty to Ladybank closed in 1957 and was used to store redundant wagons and coaches. (Alexander T. G. Wilson, Iain A. H. Smith collection)

Two photographs taken from the A92 bridge across the Fife & Kinross Railway, west of Ladybank, showing, on the left, one of the Sentinel steam railcars that were used on the line in the 1930s, and, on the right, Hunslet 0-6-0 shunter (Class 05) D2579 shunting redundant wagons in 1962. (Alexander T. G. Wilson, Iain A. H. Smith collection)

Auchtermuchty station staff pose for the camera in this photograph from the early twentieth century. (Author's collection)

North British Railway D34 Glen Class 4-4-0 No. 256 *Glen Douglas* has just arrived and run round its train, and is now ready to leave Auchtermuchty for Kinross Junction and then along the Devon Valley line to Alloa with the April 1963 BLS/SLS Scottish Rambler railtour. (Ernie's Railway Archive)

By the time this photograph was taken in 1960, Auchtermuchty signal box had been closed for three years following the closure of the Auchtermuchty to Ladybank section of the Fife & Kinross Railway. Passenger services on the line had been withdrawn in 1950. (Tony and Nick Harden collection)

Auchtermuchty station yard, as photographed on an unknown date and from a position that today would be inside the Sterling Furniture warehouse. The goods yard would have handled a variety of materials, including castings from Ferlie's Foundry, scales from John White's and, before it closed in 1926, whisky from the Stratheden Distillery. (Michael Mason collection)

On 15 July 1950, the bridge that carried the B936 across the railway at Auchtermuchty station collapsed under the weight of a low loader carrying a mechanical excavator. The two vehicles landed on the railway below, killing the two-man crew. (Author's collection)

A J37 0-6-0 heads towards Mawcarse Junction, at Strathmiglo station, with a short freight train. Strathmiglo station still stands and has been converted into a house. (Neville Stead)

This bizarre derailment took place at Mawcarse station – not technically in Fife, but on the Fife & Kinross Railway – in March 1947 when three 0-6-0 tender locomotives propelling a snowplough became derailed after the snowplough caught a broken fishplate and lifted the track as it passed through the station. (John MacDonald collection, courtesy of David Crichton)

Taken from the top of Ladybank maltings, a B1 4-6-0 departs Ladybank and is about to pass Ladybank South signal box, starting the climb to Lochmuir summit. In the foreground are the Fife & Kinross line and the permanent way yard. (Alexander T. G. Wilson, Iain A. H. Smith collection)

In its very smart livery, a GNER HST crosses the River Eden shortly after passing Ladybank with a morning Aberdeen to London Kings Cross service in June 2000. GNER were the first holders of the East Coast franchise at rail privatisation. (Author)

During February 1968,
English Electric Type 5
Deltic (Class 55) D9004
Queen's Own Highlander
was employed on air-brake
crew training and is seen here
about to pass Forthar Bridge
on the climb to Lochmuir.
The loading bank to the
right was where lime from
the Forthar Lime Works
was transferred from the
works' tramway to railway
wagons waiting in a short
siding. (Author)

EWS Class 37 No. 37428
was named *Royal Scotsman*
and painted in matching
livery to work this prestigious
train. EWS were the first
operators of this train after
privatisation and it is seen
here at Forthar Bridge,
heading from Dundee to
Edinburgh, on the fourth and
final day of the Classic Tour
in August 2003. (Author)

An unidentified Class 47
approaches Falkland Road at
the head of a London-bound
express in April 1978. By
the following year HSTs
had taken over these
trains. (Author)

Falkland Road station, which was actually closer to Freuchie, closed to passengers in 1958 and is seen here in 1960, still looking quite tidy. There were once plans to build a line from here to Falkland and Strathmiglo to link up with the Fife & Kinross Railway, but this never happened. (Jim Balnaves)

An excerpt from the Falkland Road signal box train register for 2 March 1953 shows signalmen John MacDonald, on the day shift, and Arthur Fairfield, taking over at 2 p.m. to do the back shift. Entries of note are two movements in and out of the goods yard and among the locomotives noted is A3 Pacific No. 60100 *Spearmint*, the long-time mount of Haymarket driver and railway writer Norman McKillop. (John MacDonald collection, courtesy of Jim Balnaves)

A Class 25 approaches Falkland Road working a Perth to Edinburgh service in May 1980. (Author)

A HST in InterCity Swallow livery passes Falkland Road in May 1990. The goods yard and signal box had closed in 1964, followed by the removal of the platforms in 1966. The adjoining house was occupied into the 1980s while the rest of the building became a farm store. The whole building was demolished in 1998. (Author)

One of the short-lived Clayton Type 1s (Class 17), No. D8529 passes under Kirkforthar Feus bridge in April 1971 and climbs the last few yards to Lochmuir summit with a ballast train, which probably originated at Clatchard Craig Quarry at Newburgh. (David Crichton)

On a fine summer's morning in June 1970, Brush Type 4 (Class 47) No. 1973 passes Lochmuir loop with the Aberdeen sleeper; a much longer train than the four coaches that run nowadays. (David Crichton)

Moving on to a fine summer's evening in May 1978, an unidentified Class 40 heads a northbound cement train past Class 37 No. 37042, which is standing in Lochmuir loop with an engineer's train. The signal box and loop closed in 1980. (Author)

Newly preserved and restored A4 Pacific No. 4498 *Sir Nigel Gresley* approaches Lochmuir summit with a returning Glasgow to Aberdeen railtour in May 1967. The train had headed north via Perth and the Strathmore route. This was the locomotive's first trip to Scotland after being preserved. (David Crichton)

A4 Pacific No. 60009 *Union of South Africa* brings the LCGB Forth & Tay railtour past Lochmuir signal box in June 1975. The tour had originated at Crewe, with No. 9 heading it from Edinburgh to Dundee via Fife and returning via Perth and Stirling. (David Crichton)

Taken from Lochmuir signal box, A2 Pacific No. 60528 *Tudor Minstrel* tops Lochmuir summit with an Edinburgh-bound express, probably having made light work of the climb from Ladybank. This Dundee-based locomotive was a regular sight in Fife. (David Crichton)

On a dull autumn day in 1965, No. 60052 *Prince Palatine*, one of the last two A3 Pacifics still in service – the other being No. 60041 *Salmon Trout* – passes Lochmuir with a short fitted freight. Both locomotives were out of service by the end of the year. (David Crichton)

In the normal unkempt condition for one of these locomotives, WD 2-8-0 No. 90441 slogs up the climb from Markinch to Lochmuir summit – the highest point on the main line through Fife – with a northbound freight. (David Crichton)

With not a hint of exhaust on what must have been a hot summer's day, B1 4-6-0 No. 61180 approaches Lochmuir signal box with what could possibly be a returning Dundee to Blackpool holiday special. Even as late as 1966 these trains were still steam-hauled and used a mixture of coaching stock, as seen here. (David Crichton)

When it was once possible to sit behind the driver and watch the line ahead, the windows of a DMU frame Markinch Junction signal box and signal perfectly in this view from July 1977. (David Christie)

With Birrell of Markinch lorries in the background, Class 06 shunter No. 06008 draws a couple of empty wagons out of the Markinch & District Co-Op's coal yard in April 1980. There appears to be what looks like an unofficial driver, and note the pipe-smoking shunter on the far front step of the locomotive. (Bruce Galloway)

A Hunslet (Class 05) 0-6-0 shunter propels a brake van up the Auchmuty branch from the Tullis Russell Paper Mills towards Markinch in the mid-1960s. In the background is Auchmuty Junction with the Leslie branch heading off to the left, across Balbirnie viaduct. (J. M. Boyes/J. W. Armstrong trust, courtesy of Graham Maxtone)

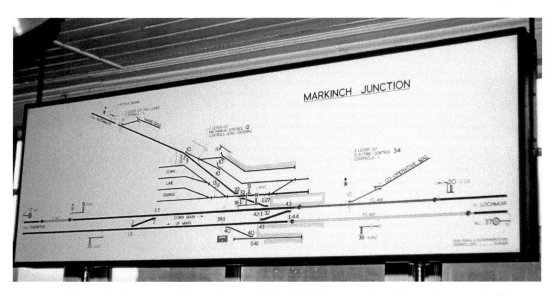

The track diagram and lever frame of Markinch Junction signal box, photographed in 1975 – five years before closure. On the track diagram can be seen the Co-Op siding, the Auchmuty branch and Haig's sidings. The forty-five-lever frame had by this time sixteen white, out of use levers. (Author)

Markinch goods shed was home to A4 Pacific No. 60009 *Union of South Africa* from 1974 to 1994, apart from a brief spell at Thornton in 1990–91. The locomotive is seen in these two photographs prepared and ready to set off the following day to Edinburgh; top, to work a train to Aberdeen and return in April 1981, and bottom, to work to Dundee and return in October 1981. (Author)

With a wreath attached, Class 08 shunter No. 08761 has just brought the last ever wagon up the Auchmuty branch from the Tullis Russell Paper Mill. Much of the mill's raw materials had been delivered by rail over the years, but this came to an end with the withdrawal of the Speedlink Service in 1991 and the later closing of the branch, which is now a cycle path. (Jim Balnaves)

Saved by my father when it was removed, this cast-iron plate was once fixed to a sleeper at a point in the Tullis Russell Paper Mills yard where the mill's private sidings began. (Author's collection)

The Leslie branch, running from Markinch Junction to Leslie, opened in 1861 and was closed to passengers in 1932. Freight continued until 1967, primarily to Fettykil Paper Mill, and J38 0-6-0 No. 65921 is shown here having just arrived at Leslie station with a train of coal for the mill. It will now reverse its train across the Glenrothes to Leslie road and into the mill's sidings. (Robin Barbour, courtesy of Bruce McCartney)

J37 0-6-0 No. 64595 climbs up the Fettykil Paper Mill siding towards Leslie station with empty wagons on a snowy day in the 1960s. The Leslie branch is now the Boblingen Cycle Way, named after Glenrothes' German twin town. (Marshall Dickson)

Fife's miniature Crewe, Thornton Junction, had lines radiating from the main line to the Fife coast, Methil and Dunfermline, as well as the station, numerous sidings and the Balgonie coal mine. Thornton Junction once had six signal boxes, but by the time these photographs were taken in the 1970s these had been reduced to only three. All the signal boxes closed in 1980.

Top: Thornton station signal box with a Class 47 passing on a southbound express. (David Crichton)

Middle: Thornton West, which was situated at the west end of the triangle and near to the site of the original Thornton engine sheds. (Author)

Bottom: Thornton South, with the Thornton breakdown train, topped and tailed by a Class 26 and Class 20, attending to a derailed wagon. (David Crichton)

V3 2-6-2T No. 67669 stands at Thornton Junction station's Down main platform at the head of a two-coach train in the 1950s. This Dunfermline-based locomotive was built in 1938 as a V1 and was converted to a V3, with a higher pressure boiler, in 1943. The signal box beyond the train is Thornton Central. (David Crichton collection)

In June 1957, Class D34 No. 62478 *Glen Quoich* stands in the Dunfermline dock platform at Thornton Junction station. Note the incorrect class number painted on the buffer beam. The station was constantly sinking due to mine subsidence and therefore had to be raised up every so often. It closed in October 1969, at the same time as the Leven line. (George Bett)

Taken from what would be at the time the A92 bridge across the railway at Thornton, B1 4-6-0 No. 61102 approaches with a coal train, past what is now the site of Glenrothes with Thornton station, in September 1966. The tall stone building above the locomotive would have once held a beam engine for pumping water out of a coal mine. It has recently been incorporated into a small housing development. (David Christie)

Looking from the other side of the bridge, again in September 1966, WD 2-8-0 No. 90020 passes Thornton Weights signal box, which controlled access to the engine sheds. In the left background are the sheds and coaling plant and to the right is the ill-fated Rothes Colliery, which opened in 1957 and closed five years later due to geological problems and severe flooding. (David Christie)

Thornton's engine shed (62A in BR days) had the fifth largest allocation of locomotives in Scotland in the 1950s. It was opened in 1933. At the west end of the shed stands the now preserved K4 2-6-0 No. 61994 *The Great Marquess*. The five locomotives that made up this class spent most of their lives on the West Highland line and were transferred to Thornton in 1959. They remained in service until 1961. (Iain A. H. Smith collection)

Shafts of light shine through the roof onto J37 0-6-0 No. 64602, a WD 2-8-0 and a J38 0-6-0 at rest on two of Thornton shed's six lines. (Marshall Dickson)

Built in 1900, J36 0-6-0 No. 65345 stands under Thornton shed's coaling plant in the mid-1960s. This veteran locomotive lasted until the end of steam in Scotland. It was known in its later years as 'Doctor Finlay's Engine' after it played a starring role in the popular BBC medical drama *Doctor Finlay's Casebook*. (David Crichton)

Two photographs of locomotives with different futures ahead of them are seen stored at Thornton in May 1968. While A2 Pacific No. 60532 *Blue Peter*, on the left, would head south to Doncaster for restoration and a new life in preservation, NBL Type 2 D6126, on the right, would head for the scrapyard along with other members of its class that were stored at Thornton at this time. (Author)

Class 20 No. 20221 heads an empty MGR train onto the Westfield branch in 1983. It is on its way to the Westfield opencast mine where the train will be loaded with coal for Longannet power station. This line originally continued on to Kelty via the Lochore causeway. (John Cumming)

Class 27 No. 27025 stands in front of the Thornton servicing depot, which opened in 1984 and was situated at the east end of Thornton marshalling yard. The Westfield branch can be seen curving away to the right, under Strathore Road, in this view from April 1987. (Bruce Galloway)

By 2007 the servicing depot was surplus to requirements and became home to John Cameron's two locomotives, K4 2-6-0 No. 61994 *The Great Marquess* and A4 Pacific No. 60009 *Union of South Africa*. They are seen here, having just arrived at their new home in April 2007. (Author)

Beautifully framed by the footbridge, a Class 101 DMU arrives at Cardenden station with a service to Edinburgh Waverley in March 1975. This is a scene that has changed out of all recognition; not only has the station building gone, but the platform has been repositioned. (Peter Rose)

With Bowhill Colliery prominent in the background, a Class 101 DMU departs Lochgelly station with an Edinburgh Waverley to Cardenden service in March 1975. Like Cardenden, Lochgelly's station buildings have since been demolished and replaced with bus shelter accommodation. (Peter Rose)

Standard Class 4 2-6-0 No. 76109 passes Lumphinnans East Junction with a coal train from Thornton yard to Alloa yard. It is signalled to take the line through Cowdenbeath station rather than the avoiding line. The line to the left goes to Lumphinnans North Junction and Kelty. (Marshall Dickson)

In deplorable external condition – apart from the cabside, which has been cleaned to apply the yellow stripe barring the locomotive from overhead electrified lines – A3 Pacific No. 60041 *Salmon Trout* passes Lumphinnans East with a Dundee to Edinburgh Millerhill fitted freight. (Marshall Dickson)

A Black 5 4-6-0 on snowplough duty pauses at Cowdenbeath station during the severe winter of 1962–63. (Marshall Dickson)

This Edinburgh Waverley-bound Class 101 DMU has just passed under the M90 motorway and is about to pass Halbeath signal box and level crossing in this view from April 1975. The photographer is standing beside Halbeath station, which closed in 1930 but survives to this day. (Peter Rose)

The driver of Class 25 No. 25087 walks back to check his train – all one wagon and brake van of it – in Townhill yard, Dunfermline, in May 1979. The buildings to the right are Townhill Wagon Works, part of which became a motive power depot following the closure of the Thornton and Dunfermline engine sheds in 1969. (Peter Rose)

Left: Townhill Junction signal box would remain open for one more year after this photograph was taken in May 1979. It controlled the lines to Dunfermline Upper and Dunfermline Lower. This is now the site of Queen Margaret station. (Peter Rose)

Right: J38 0-6-0 No. 65903 running tender-first with a brake van, on the main line, passes Dunfermline engine shed yard. (Robin Barbour courtesy of Bruce McCartney)

Dunfermline engine sheds were situated to the east of Dunfermline Upper station and replaced an earlier building that was next to the station. Its shed code in BR days was 62C. In this interior view, a J37 0-6-0, Standard Class 4 2-6-0 No. 76110, a B1 4-6-0 and a barrow are in residence. (Robin Barbour, courtesy of Bruce McCartney)

An early 1950s view of D33 4-4-0 No. 62464 in Dunfermline engine shed yard. This locomotive was withdrawn in 1953. The signal box to the left is Dunfermline Upper. (Ernie's Railway Archive)

In the superb condition it was kept in its last year, J36 0-6-0 No. 65288 stands awaiting its next duty at Dunfermline shed. This locomotive was the shed master's 'pet' and he found work for it every day so as to put off its withdrawal from service. When it was finally withdrawn in June 1967, after seventy years' service, it was the oldest working locomotive on British Railways and, along with Thornton classmate No. 65345, was the last Scottish-based steam locomotive in service. (Robin Balfour, courtesy of Bruce McCartney)

Standing forlorn at Dunfermline shed on a cold March day in 1967, J38 0-6-0 No. 65929, with its dome cover and front number plate removed, awaits its fate. Withdrawal would come a few weeks later, although it's doubtful whether it worked again after this photograph was taken. (Author)

On a number of occasions in May 1968, A3 Pacific No. 4472 *Flying Scotsman* worked trains north to Edinburgh and Dunfermline, most famously recreating its non-stop run from London to Edinburgh on the fortieth anniversary of this event. Dunfermline shed and the nearby triangle were used to service and turn the locomotive on each of these occasions. The famous locomotive is seen here at Dunfermline shed. (David Crichton)

Photographed in 1975, seven years after it closed to passengers, Dunfermline Upper station was the original terminus of the line from Thornton, which opened in 1849 – the line later being extended to Alloa and Stirling, opening in 1850–52. Dunfermline's art deco fire station can be seen in the distance, which is the only thing that remains of this view. (Peter Rose)

Seen earlier in Townhill yard and photographed here from the brake van, Class 25 No. 25087 with its one coal wagon passes Dunfermline Upper yard in May 1979. (Peter Rose)

Oakley station closed to passengers in October 1968 when all passenger services were withdrawn from the Dunfermline to Stirling line. The years until 1975 haven't been kind to it as this photograph shows, the station contrasting sharply with the distinctive 1950s signal box. (Peter Rose)

Comrie Colliery, which opened in 1938, was connected to the Dunfermline to Stirling line by a branch from Oakley. It had a fleet of steam locomotives that worked into the 1970s. Here, one of its Austerity 0-6-0 saddle tanks stands outside the locomotive shed in April 1976. (Peter Rose)

An Austerity saddle tank shunts wagons behind the colliery buildings at Comrie Colliery in December 1976. (Peter Rose)

Austerity 0-6-0ST No. 19 shunts coal wagons at Comrie Colliery in February 1975. Built by Hunslet of Leeds in 1954, this locomotive is now preserved in operational condition at the SRPS's Bo'ness & Kinneil Railway. (Peter Rose)

Built by Hunslet of Leeds in 1954, and Giesl ejector fitted, Austerity 0-6-0ST No. 5 heads for Oakley with a coal train from Comrie Colliery at the A907 level crossing – 'The White Gates' – in Comrie village in March 1976. Like No. 19 this locomotive is also at the Bo'ness & Kinneil Railway, but is awaiting restoration. (Peter Rose)

No. 19 is seen again in February 1975, passing the White Gates signal box, heading for Oakley. Note the shunter's pole carried on the buffer beam. (Peter Rose)

Approaching Bogside station at the head of a ballast train in December 1966 is J38 0-6-0 No. 65934. The station closed to passengers in 1958, as did the line west from here in 1979. Today the line is the Dunfermline & West Fife cycleway. The signal box survives and if you look in the bushes you will find the waiting room too. (David Christie)

A WD 2-8-0 and J36 0-6-0 running light pass Bogside on their way to Dunfermline in September 1966. The section of line from Bogside to Oakley closed in 1982, and, following the closure of Comrie Colliery, from Oakley to Dunfermline in 1987. (David Christie)

J38 0-6-0 No. 65905 takes water at Dunfermline Lower station, now Dunfermline Town, in June 1962 while at the head of the RCTS/SLS joint Scottish railtour. This ten-day tour covered all of Scotland and this locomotive was used for most of the Fife lines the tour visited. Here it is about to leave for Elbowend Junction and the Charlestown branch. (Ernie's Railway Archive)

Dunfermline Lower signal box, with the station behind, as photographed in April 1976. The overall roof canopies on the far platform, which can be seen in the 1962 photograph, have been removed and replaced with bus shelter accommodation in the intervening years. (Peter Rose)

Charlestown Junction is where trains heading south from Dunfermline take either the line to Rosyth and the Forth Bridge or the line to Kincardine and Stirling via Elbowend Junction, where the line to Charlestown branched off. The junction signal box is seen here in September 1978. (Peter Rose)

J36 0-6-0 No. 65288 takes the Stirling line at Charlestown Junction with a Railway Society of Scotland brake van railtour in October 1966. The locomotive is in superb condition, much of the cleaning probably having been done by members of the Dunfermline High School Railway Society. (Marshall Dickson)

The Station Charlestown

Originally a wagon way running from Charlestown to Dunfermline and dating back to 1834, the Charlestown branch became a railway proper in 1894 following realignment and the easing of gradients. Fundamentally a mineral-carrying line, it only carried passengers until 1926. This old postcard shows the passenger station when it was still open. The line still exists, although it is disconnected from the network at Elbowend Junction. (Tony and Nick Harden collection)

A B1 4-6-0 and brake van head east at Culross on the Dunfermline to Alloa via Kincardine line. The line ran from Elbowend Junction to Kincardine Junction, east of Alloa, where it joined the direct Dunfermline to Stirling line and was fully open by 1903. Still open today, it sees little use since the reopening of the Stirling to Alloa line and the closure of Longannet power station. (Robin Balfour, courtesy of Bruce McCartney)

Seen earlier in this book at Ladybank, A4 Pacific No. 60009 *Union of South Africa* heads downhill from Dunfermline to Inverkeithing with its main line return special in May 1973. At Inverkeithing a diesel locomotive took over for the rest of the journey to Edinburgh, as steam locomotives were not permitted in Edinburgh at this time. (Neville Stead, No. 60009 locomotive support crew collection)

Passengers head past the old coach on the platform and up the steps to the road above as a Class 101 DMU departs Rosyth Halt and starts the steep climb to Dunfermline with an Edinburgh Waverley to Cowdenbeath service in March 1975. (Peter Rose)

The Francis Colliery exchange sidings stood to the north of Dysart station and in this busy scene J37 0-6-0 No. 64570 prepares to leave with a coal train as a B1 4-6-0 shunts in the background. The track to the right led down to the colliery. Visible in the distance is the once familiar sight of a W. Alexander & Sons, Fife, red double-decker bus. (Marshal Dickson)

Built in 1902, Andrew Barclay 0-4-0ST No. 3 heads up the Francis Colliery yard and away towards the colliery buildings in February 1971 with loaded coal wagons, which will ultimately be taken to Bowhill Colliery for washing. The Francis closed in 1988, never having resumed production after the 1984–85 miners' strike. Today, only the headframe remains, as a monument to this once great industry. (Author)

Andrew Barclay 0-4-0ST No. 29 of 1908 vintage heads through the colliery buildings, left, and takes a rest, right, while a Clayton Type 1 (Class 17) shunts in the colliery yard in March 1971. No. 29 has recently moved from the Preston Grange Mining Museum to Shed 47 at the Scottish Bus Museum, Lathamond, for its restoration to working order. (Author)

By 1975, when this
photograph was taken,
Dysart signal box
stood alone, the station
which closed in 1969
having been demolished.
The box closed in
1980. (Author)

A2 Pacific No. 60532 *Blue Peter* creates an impressive sight as it rounds the curve on the
approach to Dysart station, on the climb from Kirkcaldy, with an Edinburgh to Aberdeen
express in August 1966. *Blue Peter* was withdrawn from service a few months later.
(Marshall Dickson)

Kirkcaldy once had three stations, Dysart, Sinclairtown and Kirkcaldy, which are all seen here in period postcards from the early twentieth century. Only Kirkcaldy remains, but with modern buildings. Dysart and Sinclairtown both closed in 1969. (Tony and Nick Harden collection)

In May 1936 the LNER held an exhibition of locomotives and rolling stock at Sinclairtown goods yard, Kirkcaldy. Star exhibits were P2 2-8-2 No. 2001 *Cock O' The North*, top, with one of Kirkcaldy's many linoleum factories behind, and A4 Pacific No. 2511 *Silver King*, bottom. No. 2001 was one of a class of six built to haul the heavy Edinburgh to Aberdeen trains and No. 2511 was one of the original four A4s built to haul the Silver Jubilee express between London and Newcastle. A replica of *Cock O' The North* is currently under construction. (Iain A. H. Smith collection)

As late as February 1975, when this photograph was taken, Kinghorn station was still lit by gas lamps. This lamp is mounted on top of an Edinburgh & Northern Railway lamp post, which would date back to the opening of the line in 1847. (Peter Rose)

Two photographs taken between Kinghorn and Burntisland show, top, one of Dundee shed's well-kept V2 2-6-2s, No. 60973, coasting downhill to Burntisland with a Dundee to Millerhill fitted freight, and, bottom, a B1 4-6-0, No. 61344, climbing away from Burntisland with a northbound passenger train. (Marshall Dickson)

An unidentified Class 26 passes Burntisland Junction signal box in March 1975. The box controlled access to Burntisland docks – a busy place, with regular shipments of bauxite arriving for the nearby British Aluminium Works. Burntisland dockyard also had its own sidings. (Author)

Edinburgh St Margarets-based V2 2-6-2 No. 60846 stands in Burntisland sidings with a train of empty cement wagons bound for Oxwellmains Cement Works at Dunbar. (John S. McCracken, courtesy of Ian R. W. McCracken)

Burntisland had a small engine shed, originally a round house, which was a sub shed of Thornton. Here, with the fireman keeping an eye on the water level and the driver ready to turn it off, Thornton-based J36 No. 65345 takes water. (John S. McCracken courtesy of Ian R. W. McCracken)

Glasgow Eastfield shed's Standard Class 5 Caprotti 4-6-0 No. 73146 stands in Burntisland yard. It had probably worked to Burntisland with empty Presflow wagons, which can be seen behind the locomotive, from the British Aluminium smelter at Fort William, which would now be re-loaded with alumina for a return trip. (John S. McCracken, courtesy of Ian R. W. McCracken)

This postcard commemorates the Burntisland derailment, which occurred on 14 April 1914. It involved North British Atlantic locomotive No. 872 *Auld Reekie*, hauling an Aberdeen-bound express, colliding with the locomotive of a goods train that was reversing its train out of the way of the express. The resulting collision caused No. 872 and the leading coaches of its train to crash onto Burntisland Links, below. A signalling error was to blame for the accident. (John McDonald collection, courtesy of David Crichton)

Preserved D49 4-4-0 Shire Class No. 246 *Morayshire* rounds the sharp curve at Burntisland with a SRPS Falkirk to Dundee railtour in April 1981. The last of its class in service, this locomotive was saved from the scrapyard by Ian Fraser, who, following restoration, presented it to the Royal Scottish Museum. Still owned by the museum, *Morayshire* has been under the care of the SRPS since 1974. (Marshall Dickson)

The British Aluminium Company's works at Burntisland was rail-connected and, up to the early 1970s, had its own fleet of steam locomotives. BAC No. 1, a Pecket 0-4-0ST built in 1915, shunts wagons at the works. This locomotive moved to the Lochty Private Railway in 1973 and is now at Bridge of Dun on the Caledonian Railway. (David Crichton)

BAC No. 2, another Pecket 0-4-0ST, this time built in 1921, stands outside its shed. Upon withdrawal in 1972 it was acquired by the Bulmer Railway Centre at Hereford, who named it *Pectin*. Still carrying this name, it is now at the Yeovil Railway Centre in Somerset. (David Crichton)

Two workers pose with BAC No. 3, an Andrew Barclay-built 0-4-0ST dating from 1937. Presented to the SRPS, it is now at the Bo'ness & Kinneil Railway. Diesel locomotives took over from the steam fleet and the works closed in 2002 after eighty-five years. The site is now a housing estate. (David Crichton)

Left: Newbiggin signal box controlled access to the aluminium works and is seen here having been photographed from a passing Class 101 DMU while working an Edinburgh to Dundee service in June 1975.

Right: Aberdour signal box is seen here, when still open in March 1975. Closed in 1980, the box still stands and was recently restored. It is now used as a pottery studio. (Author)

Two smartly dressed enthusiasts watch B1 4-6-0 No. 61343 departing Inverkeithing station with an Edinburgh to Dundee service in August 1965. The coal in the tender doesn't look to be the best and will probably give the fireman problems on the gradients ahead. (David Christie)

A3 Pacific No. 4472 *Flying Scotsman* departs Inverkeithing station with a Stockton to Dunfermline and return railtour in May 1968. Fitted with two tenders by this time, the second, water-carrying tender was coupled to No. 60009 *Union of South Africa* before being acquired and modified for No. 4472. Upon preservation, No. 60009 received the tender coupled to No. 60004 *William Whitelaw*. This tender, when built in 1929, was coupled to experimental locomotive No. 10000 *The Hush Hush*. (Matthew Mather)

Director Class D11 4-4-0 No. 62677 *Edie Ochiltree* comes off the Rosyth Dockyard branch at Inverkeithing South with a workers' train, which is bound for Kirkcaldy. (Robin Balfour, courtesy of Bruce McCartney)

Thomas Wards of Inverkeithing were better known for scrapping ships – notably the *Titanic*'s sister ship *Olympic* and the second *Mauretania* – but in the 1960s they also scrapped steam locomotives, including three Britannia Class Pacifics, Nos 70004 *William Shakespeare*, 70014 *Iron Duke* and 70035 *Rudyard Kipling*. Here, one of the trio meets its end. (Marshall Dickson)

J37 0-6-0 No. 64572 stands at Rosyth dockyard platform at the head of a workers' train. The Rosyth branch, although rarely used, is still intact and the signal box seen in the distance still stands. (Ernie's Railway Archive)

With banking assistance from a J37 0-6-0, a B1 4-6-0 heads a heavy Burntisland to Fort William alumina train, which is seen approaching Jamestown viaduct on the steep climb to the Forth Bridge in the early 1960s. Prominent on the skyline is the then new Forth Road Bridge. (Marshall Dickson)

V2 2-6-2 No. 60813 is a superb sight as it crosses Jamestown viaduct with a southbound passenger train in 1966. This Dundee-based locomotive was fitted with a smoke deflector rim around the side and rear of its chimney. (Marshall Dickson)

Moving on a few yards, V2 2-6-2 No. 60813 is seen again at Jamestown, this time entering the deep rock cutting before North Queensferry Tunnel with a southbound passenger train, in 1966. (Marshall Dickson)

An official invitation to the opening of the Forth Bridge by the Prince of Wales on Tuesday 4 March 1890 from the Forth Bridge Railway Company. The company comprised the North British, Great Northern, North Eastern and Midland Railway companies. (Kenneth J. Williamson collection)

This early twentieth-century postcard depicts five views of the Forth Bridge. The bottom right view is of North British Atlantic No. 868 *Aberdonian*, the first of the class, which was built in 1906, and is appropriately seen going to Aberdeen. (Matthew Mather collection)

Two photographs taken on a misty day on the Forth in May 1973. On the left, an unidentified Class 20 approaching Forth Bridge North signal box, while on the right, with the Forth Bridge towering behind, a Class 101 DMU approaches North Queensferry station with an Edinburgh to Kirkcaldy service. (Author)

In Strathclyde PTE livery, a Class 101 DMU crosses the Forth Bridge in the 1990s. This image was taken while the photographer was on an official walk across the bridge. (John McDonald courtesy of David Crichton)

This volume finishes where it started, at Thornton engine shed. WD 2-8-0 No. 90628 raises steam in the shed in the 1960s, with two J37 0-6-0s for company. (Marshall Dickson)